through the veil

A POETRY COLLECTION TO SOOTHE
THE GRIEF-LADEN SOUL

BONNIE MCCALL

Printed in the United States of America
Published in Hellertown, PA
Cover design and images by Noelle McCall

ISBN 978-8-89420-018-7

To my brothers John, R. Del, and Gordon
This book is dedicated to all the lonely people who are grieving the loss of someone who was so special, so very loved.
May you go through the veil to peace, love, and joy.

January

The ice cold rain
Falls from the sky,
Gray and uninterrupted.
No wind,
No breeze,
An effortless drizzle on my face.

And I know you are speaking ever so gently,
Ever so tingly on my warm, weathered skin.
You speak through these droplets,
Tears on my face.

But I cannot hear a word,
Only the years and years of knowledge we shared.
You wanted the burden of saving others
And freely accepted the cost,
A cost higher than you could pay.

The icy rain falls on warm earth.
I cannot hear your voice
Nor hold you in my frozen arms.
Brother and sister,
Lost in the chasm of mother and father.

Divine and human,
Goddess and god,
Passion and violence,
Love and pain,
Snow and rain,
Fall on this warm earth.
I spin and spin,
But you are gone,
And it feels
Comfortless.

Yet the cold ice melts on my face
Again and again and again.

Grief

The night mist
Wraps around the light post
That lights the back alley
In a mysterious grip
That came from fingers of fog
Down from the sky above.
It looks like an orb,
An orb that overpowers my mind
And I feel like my soul is exposed.

I don't want to be alone on this path.
I don't want to lose anymore.
I cling to the illusion that someone is there.

I am afraid
That the mist of this night
Will extinguish the light
From the post that is engulfed
By the fingers of fog
That encase the eyes of my mind,
An orb of light that is snuffed
By the harsh words I encountered today.

For a moment,
Allow me to be sad.
For a moment,
Grief.

The Air in Your Eyes

I could breathe in the air
I saw in your eyes,
Knowing well that it would take me away,
Like a zeppelin floating above the Earth.

We could travel together, you and I,
With our hearts untouched by worry, pressureless.
There would be no more hopeless encounters
Nor grievous plays on the stage of life.

I watched from the balcony with lorgnettes framed in gold,
As you, my thespian hero, played out your victorious role.
Champion of love and goodness,
Yet crucified by mortal laws.
My role, to clap you onward.
And, as each act finished,
The crimson velvet curtain came down
On the wooden stage, polished but worn,
Each prop was repositioned.
The air was tinted with the haze of a well-perfumed theater.
Musk and sandalwood blend
With the sweat of actors rushing about in haste.
Your lines are immaculately polished and delivered with perfection.

At the end, I was wrapped by spirit and catapulted into your final act.
I permitted you to exit my realm,
And the villain swung a victorious sword
In self-righteous grandeur. *Enfin, la fin!*
I crumple.
My skirts, layer on layer, swallow me
As I fade into numbness and disbelief.

There is air inside my eyes now.
I breathe the essence daily of your beautiful, hazel eyes.
Your soft voice echoes the multiple lines
We practiced together for this performance.

I am left behind with a deep, gnawing ache
That tenderly awaits our reunion.

Some do not understand this deep connection.
We are soul travelers,
Pursuing, purging, and resurrecting one another.
As we inspire each breath,
We breathe in the image of each other's eyes.
We see eternity.
And I, left alone here, am but a breath away from you.

BONNIE MCCALL

Phone Call

I saw you today, peeking out of a cloud
As I drove over that hill on a country road.
The sky was full,
Fluffy cumulus heaps
Competing with mountain ranges on earth,
Stating comparatively
That solidness had no edge on the creative landscape
Of its empyrean realm.
There was a spot above me
Where I saw you,
Sitting and watching,
Then disappearing.
I ran home in my usual angst,
Feeling like nothingness
From that fresh biting ache of loss.
Inside I wondered how many times you felt that way
And wondered why you loved me,
So filled with flaws.
I dialed your number just to hear your voice.
And I dialed your number
Just to remember me.
Your recorded voice played inside
The air between my lungs.
Although your life was erased one month ago.
I can't remember who I am.
You always helped to ground me.
Now I am grounded without you.

A Thousand Pieces

When I break into a thousand pieces,
Gather me up
In love.
And when I'm thrown into the fire so hated,
Cool me with your balm.
And when I lose my sight
And feel so aimless,
Shepherd me with care,
For I am just a fragment of your soul space.

So mend me,
Hover over me,
Speak gently in my ear.
Mother me with soft and gentle phrases.
I long to hear your voice.

It's been too long.
I'm broken glass
A thousand pieces from my home.

BONNIE MCCALL

Cold Conversation

The bark of the golden retriever
Pierces through the night.
It is sharp and penetrating,
Unlike any sound he previously made,
Alerting all to his need.

He rushes inside and curls up, eyes guardedly watching the door.
Night filters through the quiet.
Sleep attempts to grab my mind,
But I am reminded of the train
That hauntingly rumbles through northern New York
Every night at four a.m.
A whistle shrills in the distance,
Lost and entangled with spirits
Pulling and grasping at metallic wheels,
Screaming the cries of ancient betrayals and
Dark mysteries hidden in the cold north.
Icy fingers extract dreams from children,
Awakening mothers to comfort them
From the fear the sounds arouse.

Books are aligned in corner racks in every small store,
Filled with stories
Of haunted buildings, ghostly murders, and fragmented lives.
An ambience of mystery lingers in rafters of old buildings
Of frozen little towns sprinkled near Canada,
Entities struggling for survival.

A flash of light in memory,
Talking with you on a cold winter night.
Chilly air seeped through the windowsill and a shield of ice,
But you warmed me with childhood memories.

Only you could break the spell that northern spirits cast on me.
Both of us were broken by different circumstances,
Both of us were tired yet bonded eternally by an unseen cord,
Paralyzed yet free,
Wholly mesmerized by our quest.

Your voice is frozen in eternity now,
While my warm retriever comforts me in wordless darkness.

Seventeen Days

I could hardly breathe,
Walking through the grocery store today,
Wondering how you made it through the past two years
Before we all knew
That you would leave us soon.

I would have helped.
I swear, I would have helped!
But the basket was leaking from the bottom,
And the water-damaged ceiling
Would never stop.
Catching droplets of life
Becomes senseless in this everchanging game.

Buddha would not have been happy if
I put a solid bucket there,
Beneath the ceiling of endless drizzle.
Age to age, lessons were taught.
We cannot fix what was not meant to be fixed
Nor heal the one who does not want to be healed.

I can't breathe because I do not know
How much I should have known or done.
How much is enough in the language of love?

How much is too much to ask?
You could not ask.

Do you remember me
Trying to breathe for you,
But drowning with you?

BONNIE MCCALL

Sadness

The night is so damp,
Dark, and misty.
I glance up at the moon, three-quarters in size.
An aura surrounds its reflective light.
A black-and-white exposure,
Like an old film,
Penetrates the distance around it,
So beyond my reach,
But not beyond the image it paints on the night sky.
The tears in my brain match the mistiness
Of the darkness around me,
And I feel like I could disappear into its sad, cool vapor.
As the frigid night around me seeps into my soul,
I see that I am just walking on the water of life,
Waiting for love to boost me up into the beautiful atmosphere above,
Where a different kind of love
Melts the darkness and
Warms the wax
Of the candle that composes me.
I am an actor on this planet,
An avatar,
Kneeling at a *prie-dieu*
To listen to your wisdom flame,
A grand candelabra in front of me.
Slowly, the altar servers
One by one extinguish the candles.
The curling smoke from the flame
Drifts upward to fill
The face of the moon,
White on black on white.

BONNIE MCCALL

Overgrown

The bushes next door
In the uninhabited house
Are overgrown.
One is green with pretty white flowers.
They are all tangled together in a web of mystery.
The bushes and trees occlude the doorways,
And I worry constantly that unseen dangers are harbored there.
In this dense thicket of sad neglect,
There is a tree silhouette behind the house.
A dead tree that lets squirrels run up and down its frame,
But the birds rarely perch upon it.
I am worried that some vagabond will enter this lonely house
And be a threat to others
Who are living in a neighboring property.
This springtime,
I heard the chirping of robins,
And even saw several baby cardinals flying into branches
Barely strong enough to hold their weight,
Then flying away to the telephone lines that border our street.
They are all gone now and avoid the dead tree.
I wonder what happened to previous owners, and one day talked
briefly with the son of the dad
Who divorced the mom
Who never sold the house.
And it's been 20 years since anyone lived inside.
And he would be afraid to enter it, he said,
Due to what might be in there.
Sadness.
Was this a bitter couple
Who let the whole world collapse
And rot?
I thought of how you were unable
To keep up your property due to heart failure.
And I thought of how your children
Struggled and struggled to maintain

The home around you.
Hours of sleeping.
No communication for weeks.
I called and called.
So did everyone.
You were embarrassed for me to come, you said.
I had no idea
That you were stranded in the house next door.

Stained Glass

Radiant April sunlight
Pierces the atmosphere like a sword
So sharp that it penetrates my thoughts
And paralyzes every atom of my being.

Chilled air,
Not warmed by these rays,
Is full of silent atoms,
Colliding, crashing into one another,
Insistent on moving forward in time,
Resurrecting newness
Through the ageless painted lead
With its old knowledge of the universe.

Alpha and omega,
Beginning and end,
The morning light shifts slowly from the eastern horizon,
Clashing with the west,
And enters the stained-glass window, dancing on yellow, green, blue.
Vivid and alive,
Artists' delight
Frozen in time.
We see what we believe and hear what echoes emptily.
My heart beats
Again and again and again,
And the duality of being on this planet
Reduces me to happiness and sorrow.

I cannot see in front of me,
Because of this April light
Dancing on leaded glass.

A Shaft of Light

Slowly, with intent,
Discreet and faint at first,
Gathering grace
As it climbed the inside walls of that room,
Dust gathered to dance with the muted mystery
About to unfold.
Some motes drifted and dangled in the light,
Surging with energy.
Others searched and sifted through air in flight.
Crystalline beauty, reflecting ancient scripts of
Love danced between the shaft
Of you and I.

The dust did not settle as the light intensified.
Did you look for me that day?
My mind hopes you didn't,
But my heart knows you did.
It was all I could do to stay away,
Knowing there was so much drama already at play.

You and I know what happened,
As time folded and gently placed itself in the open drawer of eternity,
Like a soft, soft cotton made of the most brilliant threads,
Only to be worn by the highest of the high.

You radiantly rose,
A high captain,
And saluted us below,
As I danced in the dust by your side.

Field of You

The green grassy hill flows effortlessly
Behind the cracked cement roadway.
When the sun rolls up behind it
Early in the day,
A soft mist
Rises above the earth,
And sometimes
A silhouette can be seen.

Who or what is imagined in my mind?
What mysteries do my human eyes conceal or reveal?
Why did you disappear from me,
Yet leave behind this yearning love
As fragile as the mist?
Broken vessel,
Fragments of you,
Shimmer as dense as thick fog,
Like tears on a child's tender face.

Yet the tenderness of the flowing grass
Brings renewal.
A gentle comfort, the passing of the mist yearning to see
The green as
It flows into you.

You Are the Moon

The sacred moon saunters silently upward.
Hazy mist surrounds her, and she reveals her full glory.

I watch from my window, wondering why she does not cause
Others around me to watch her triumphant parade,
Going higher and higher.

None seem to pay attention to her.
Is it the constant replay of the same action,
Day after day,
Night after night,
Her quiet appearance repeating itself,
Sometimes hiding half or a quarter of herself,
Sometimes occluded by clouds,
Sometimes her wholeness disappearing completely.

Is it taken for granted that she will always be there,
Like a mother,
Hovering over her brood,
Giving only glimpses of the internal anguish she carries in the
Shadows of her face?

This we know:
She will be there, yet none watch for her,
Until she is gone.

Numb

Reflective glass,
I feel lost in the mirror.
Outside, springtime unfolds.
Inside, I still feel numb.
Although it has been months since you left
The rawness of each day continues.
I walked to my garage and would have called you to say hello.
But I remain silent, you are not here anymore.
There is an
Eye high above me.
The sun is shining brightly,
Unharnessed energy splitting
Through my crown,
Like a plant emerging from the earth,
Grounded to the center of my being.

Surrounding is the blackness of inner eternity.
I waver,
The wind is not blowing on my back but I am still bowled over.

Nothing and everything
Felt.

How can the sun shine so warmly on my head
When you have gone?

I Can't Say

I can't say a word.

The trees are capped with green silken scarves,
That flow to and fro in the breeze.
They call to me with lilting words.
They are fluffy friends and the wind playfully wrestles them.
Each branch bends to accommodate life forces.
Birds chirp endlessly,
Squirrels play like unstoppable children,
Running up trunks, jumping across branches.

When you left me,
The clouds,
The moon,
The stars,
The sun,
The grass,
The sand,
The rocks,
The sea,
The endless power of nature surrounded me
And called to me ceaselessly.

All became my blanket,
Wrapping around me like a cloud.
And, deeply, the Voice spoke to me,
"Lay back in my arms," and all would take care of me.

And I can't say a word,
For the majesty of life
Speaks.

The Race

The sun rises quietly again today.
Soft gray light, then pink, then solemn white,
Illuminates the earth.
Eyes awaken to the tired reality that more rest is needed,
But would not be possible
Again.

Forcing cells to get up,
Go onward with tasks,
Forcing feelings to submerge,
Pushing dreams to disappear so that reality
Will take over and allow itself another day
To run for the roses,
Like a racehorse well-trained,
Sleek, muscular, and black like satin.

You are my famous jockey,
Alive and humor-filled,
Willing to achieve above all others,
And to forget the sensitive soul you hide
Beneath your courageous race to the finish.

We all appear to run together,
Individual stallions,
Alone in a sea of masses.
Gunfire combusts as the sun attempts to outrun
All competitors.

We were so pushed in our youth.
It seems unnecessary now.
And when I think of our race,
Together, then separate, now alone,
I yearn to express the relentless love that remembers you.

Now, when the sun arises,
I rest in the knowledge that you are still a part of my light.
And this race toward the Greater One?
It's over.
You have won it for me.

Morning Sky

Light blue, flat, powdery-white softness floats gently overhead,
Purple-gray facing the earth, fading into a blunted horizon.

Soon the heavens will open
With torrents of words,
Flying like foreign missiles into mental templates.
But nothing computes.

Stranger in a strange land,
I seek the comfort of my dream world.
Portals to heaven open in my kitchen,
A magical staircase that leads upward,
Beyond my imagination,
Beyond the landscape that frames this earth.

Nothing is a threat to me.
I am Merlin in a fantasy, creating elements.
Only I can assign meaning to them.
Reality vanishes.
I search everywhere for you.
Where did you go?

The sky paints landscapes around me,
And together,
We fade into the morning.

Cracked Open

The neighbors
Needed to get the waterline,
Old and broken,
Fixed.
They took the sidewalk out and cracked open the earth,
Went down to the ancient line to put in a valve and fix it.
Gravel was thrown on top of the burial pit
For the precious water line,
And now we have to fix the sidewalk so it looks
Consistent with cement.
They cracked open the earth to bury you.
I was not there.
Nor was I with you
When you took your last breath.
I was cracked open
With gravel all over my brain,
Thinking what on earth had caused this terrible loss?
Was it the person who gave you morphine every hour?
Was it me running in circles figuring out boundaries
And how much ejection fraction will keep you alive?
Was it me
Who begged you to stay selfishly
Because I still need your stories,
Your wisdom,
Your spirit? Beautiful brother,
With me from day one.
Now no one on earth will ever know me as you did, and I feel
All cracked open.
All cracked open.

BONNIE MCCALL

One Raindrop Away

The summer was drenched.
Storms that passed through
Kept me one raindrop away
From you.
One raindrop away!

She has honey in her veins, she said.
My heart never beat like that.
My veins are drenched in raindrops,
An arrhythmia of sadness,
Clouds that beat perpetually through my being.

I was the most grounded person he knew, he said.
For others, I float too high.
Perhaps I need to capture some bees, and
Make some honey,
So I may feel thick with sweet riches.
Until then,
I will be
One raindrop away from you.

Sky

Speckled with sand dunes and
Wetted castles,
Housing forms and creatures
Flitting overhead
Like paper airplanes
Guided by wind,
Spitting out the manmade metal beings
And coveting the feathered few who pepper the sky.

Mesmerizing, welcoming cloudy sky,
You call daily to me.
I worship at the portal you create for me alone.
You close my mind
And open my soul,
With delicate laces that veil me from the torch,
Which blinds
But brings ultimate vision and warmth.

I dare not feel the earth.
I belong to the firmament!
You were extinguished by your twin flame,
As I bent at the altar,
Poured salt on heaven,
And resigned to write words in the sand.

Dragonfly

Everywhere,
Yesterday,
Today,
Two weeks ago,
I noticed
Dragonflies in front of me,
Flying around freely wherever I go.

One buzzed in front of my car window for minutes,
Just hovering,
Staring at me
Inside this barrier,
A metal fortress,
Chaining me to an upper room.
Prisoner to memory,
I cannot stop thinking of you.

A man strolled into the grocery store,
Happily,
Like a short, stocky man from Brigadoon in his Scottish dress,
All velvet with lace,
from a plaid past.
White hair, distinct stature,
With mannerisms all you,
Here on mother earth, breathing this air,
Buzzing everywhere like a dragonfly,
Changing form in minutes,
Haunting me.

My reality split wide open and searches,
Wondering if
The freedom you got was the freedom you sought.
Today, I walked out of an office,
And a dragonfly flew in front of me,
Escorted me several feet, then flew away.
You.

BONNIE MCCALL

Endless Vault of Heaven

An endless blue sky is above me.
The hot sun pierces through my chest
Like a knife today.
Deep ache plasters my mind,
No cobwebs exist here.
The light of loss has illuminated every corner of my being.

There is no why to be answered.
The footsteps of people who walk past me
Sound louder than ever before.
Their glances and the sound of their voices
Are muffled like a foreign language,
And I don't care to hear anything at all.
Nothing can change
Your passing.

Did the light come down and engulf you?
Did a sage angel take you by the hand and lead you off?
Was there a tunnel to travel?

I don't think you needed a tunnel.
I think you had a ticket straight up
To the highest place of honor.
I think you are as endlessly bright as the sun today.
And your love pierces my heart,
Reminding me of all the shared times we had.
More, the unshared words that you knew I heard.

The sun is too bright today.
Sky blue and endless,
Vault of Heaven,
Wind soft, engulfing, soft enough to caress my face.
Tears hot, age-old questions
Unanswered

But for when you told me
To wait and see what tomorrow might bring,
A gift you gave, yet did not receive yourself.
You were always that way,
Giving what you did not get in return.

The Highland of Heaven

The Queen of England was put to rest.
It reminds me so much of you.

Our mother longed to connect you to her adored father.
He was Scottish.
She always said that you had his same stature and gait.

The weather today suddenly turned,
Dark, sooty sky, windy gusts,
Like a day along Luskentyre.
My face is raw from the cold, dry gale.
Rushing to bring supplies to my house from the garage,
I paused and thought solidly of
Crossing the veil to heaven where you are.

Did you meet the Queen today?
Because you served so many people and cared so deeply.
A physician,
With little glory,
With no crown,
With very little retirement at the end,
All gone to others.

Do you have a castle?
A plaid to match your name?
The more I think about it, there is no caste system,
No kings and queens,
No good and bad,
No mine and yours,
No time, no separation.

Here, the wind is strong, and the sky is dark.
The rain pelts on my hair,
And I ache inside.
The heavens are vacuuming the earth,

Collecting precious gems that have aged.
Bagpipes hauntingly wail with unmatched pitch.
Medieval clay flows through my veins.
Old spirits seep from the cracks between each brick.
With darkened corridors,
Balmoral weeps her loss
With gnawing resignation.

I know you met the Queen today and danced a Ceilidh dance.

When You Sailed Away

I see your image,
All fine and formal,
Naval crisp,
Officer official, ribboned left chest,
Like a snow-capped mountain.

True captain of your sails,
Quoting W.E. Henley's "Invictus,"
You walked each word, year after year,
Hot coals beneath bare feet
Cooled by effervescent waters
As you sailed, unfailing,
To rescue me, and all those stranded or lost.

I see it all so clearly now,
Off the coast:
Me, on shore.
You, busting through miles of tormenting waves,
Distracted at night by specks upon the black sky.
Dante's Inferno flaming through my cold fingers,
The pages of words draw illustrations in my blood.
I pulse with fear,
A captive, chained embodiment of torture,
Awaiting your arrival.

You travel uncharted seas with only knowledge to guide.
It's mesmerizing how brilliantly you orchestrate the path!
I see you in the distance
And kneel, like I did weeks before you left.
I sing an unwritten melody, a chant created only for you.
And it guides you nearer and nearer,
Saving sailor of the seas!

You are close enough,
Coming landside and

Mooring your tattered shell.
You lift an intent gaze
With a chuckle!
You take my hand.
"Shall we?"
We dance on the shore until the sun rises
And swallows us.

BONNIE MCCALL

Two Empty Days

The sun is hot again,
And I cannot call you.
Sometimes you would pick up, sometimes not,
But it seemed you always called me back.

I don't think this world was made for souls like you and me.
We worked so hard to gain approval, to be loved.
Such irony.

I think of your voice and how much it meant to me,
Hearing your wisdom, stories of life, people, patients.
Like birds aligned on a telephone wire, each taught us a song.
You never stopped teaching and sharing humorous stories.
I was your captive audience for hours.

I knew I could connect with one who knew me from the beginning.
How special that is,
Knowing a full story, alpha and omega,
Sometimes judging, but you do not remember those times.
Then, in 2018, you said you were sorry, and so was I.
Few souls traverse this world
Knowing all faults, insecurities, sores, and open wounds,
And apply that special salve: friendship.

I can't say a word.
The wind blows with a soft spirit today.
The telephone wires are empty and swaying in the blur of my vision.
The sun is much too bright.
The ache inside me mounts to intolerable levels.
Yet, who would know?
Just the angels.
I whisper to them, "Please."

Everything is stuck in my throat.
My heart keeps beating.

The Red Heat of Loss

If the sun rose any crisper,
If the day began with sight,
If the breeze blew any darker,
If the summer could walk right,
If the grass grew any sadder,
If the field had rain to laugh,
If time would just stop spending down
The account of noise it spends,
I could catch my breath
And breathe.

I am a dragon that can no longer breathe.
A tamed creature,
With no flame to spew.
I have walked through loss
And felt the red heat of fire.

In the morning,
Blueness encompasses the atmosphere above.
I breathe in color around me as if it could quench
My unstoppable need
To think of you.

They threw dirt on the casket lowered.
I was not there.
She did not approve of your placement
Near the ones who brought you life.
It was all set in motion
Perfectly, as the end of a circle.
I trace the colors of eternity,
And now go around and around on the wheel of time,
Until I understand that there is no understanding
A dragon without fire,
A fire without heat,
A life without breath.

The Piles

Piles and piles of dust, web-covered, black stacked plastic boxes,
Neatly arranged in the garage of my soul,
Just waiting,
Waiting for years to be examined,
To be analyzed by a spiritual master
Lately found to have left me.

Trudging through the hot, humid day,
I begin the process that no man or god will save me from.
Days and days of work float in front of me.
Print on the page,
Names of people cared for, stories of illness and recovery.
Some passed to higher realms,
Some lingered in a distant town that no longer remembers me.

Trendy names,
Such as "Swedish Death Cleaning" and "Minimalist Living"
Cross my mind, giving energy to this daunting task.
There are webs from dust and dead spiders,
But I fearlessly brush that aside.
External dangers cannot penetrate the internal agony I feel
When documents confirm I was betrayed.

Humidity is high, and the wind starts to puff on me.
Rain pushes through as tears flood my face, and there is no lifting,
No resurrection,
No bright light to flood the garage.
There is not even lightning for such a tragic storm,
Just the slow pelting of precipitation
On a hot, humid day.
The tales are told and terminated by execution.

Tomorrow we pack and shred,
The same way they packed and shredded your sentience.
Our families line together and parade past the drops of water

That anoint this memory of time.
All that remains is an unshredded picture of you,
Now found and sheltered
In the hidden shrine of my heart.

Autumn Again

The broken branch on the tree in my backyard
Dangles in the dawning light,
While the dew sparkles on its fragile bark
With the light from the moon.
Glistening in its damaged state of mind,
It is overtaken by bewilderment.

The atmosphere is cooler now.
I hear voices rumbling all around,
Like morning fog penetrating the visual field.
Into every crevice, the seeping sound awakens nature
And beckons me to partake of
This awakening.

But I am the limb,
Still clinging to solidness, needing to free-fall into silence,
Holding onto a thread that ties me to the trunk.
I resist
With all my strength.

I believe you are still here.
I drink the elixir of reality,
Let go of myself,
And break from the life-giving trunk
While the morning mist moistens
The brown leaves that have fallen to earth.

It All Happens

It all happens
The way it is supposed to happen.
Your last call to me
Was a surprise.
Somehow, deep inside there was knowledge
That this was the last time
Your name would appear in my caller ID.
You said my name
With the same familiar sweet intonation.

There was a transparency no one else shared,
Things spoken to chosen few
Caretakers of the soul.
Like angels, we hovered over one another,
A childhood skill inbred in those of us
Who needed
To be preserved and protected.

Your wings spread like a rainbow.
Broadly watching over me,
You wrapped me with an invisible embrace,
And with your words dusted off my sadness.

BONNIE MCCALL

Into the Day

The darkness wraps around me as if a cloak.
Like a best friend, the cool night seeps into cracks,
Winding through ancient rock.
Cracks, that for centuries existed
In pyramid constructs,
Create energy vortexes.
I feel the cold dark seep into the break in my soul,
Bringing comfort.

I no longer hear or feel people with their unsettled emotions,
Flinging words at me
Like a play gun loaded with real ammunition.
I count the bullets and talk to shadows,
Searching for the validation sunlight never brought to me,
Wondering why the dark, empty hole inside of me
Still searches for home.

There is a tender voice at night, one that assures me
That feeling lost, empty, alone,
Is not real.
All is an illusion, a shadow they say,
A softness with no angles, no intentions, no hidden secrets,
Just the jagged truth.
Embracing the faults, I selfishly cling to and finally release
Into the dreamland where I won't hear daylight,
Nor feel criticism from a world that I never fit into.

I hear your voice again.
I am no longer afraid of night,
Just afraid that the day will crush me.

Please rush to me once again
And walk me home.

Unburdening

The rains have come forcefully this year.
Day after day,
Clouds of dark gray, with deep, charcoal-colored shadows,
Traverse the sky, then unburden torrents of raindrops
Upon the earth.

We scamper and run for cover.
Like missiles, the hail pierces space,
Landing loudly.

Fields are but for a moment saturated with welcome relief.
The clouds are scurrying, circling and gaining speed as they go
To their next destination.
Their mission is sure and solid,
As solid as the thirsty ground awaiting its anointing,
As solid as the mystery that shrouds the heavens
And soaks our souls with questions.
How do I navigate back home
When clouded with such heaviness, duty calling?

Coolness interferes, and we swirl,
Dropping pretense and ego,
Moving outward intensely,
Raining down energy,
Unburdening.

I create shallow pools of water with my tears.

BONNIE MCCALL

The Autumn Sun

Bright and piercing,
The autumn sun
Shone down yesterday.
Purposefully planted, it desired to have its way
And swept you up, up, and away.
Like a balloon released
By a young child.

Tracing the flight with my eyes,
I am blinded by sunlight.
Truth eclipsing my tightly gripped hand,
I want to hold on to you,
But cannot,
And you are released into mysterious heights above.

As the autumn sun
Turns crimson,
It bleeds out its life-giving ichor
On the trees behind my house.

Little Bird

Little bird, why are you singing?
Like October witches at their cauldron of spells,
The dark night bursts open at its seams, crowding and haunting,
Issuing screams!
Bring the bee balm and fairies,
Dust me, spin me in moonlight,
Repair me with amaranth.
The earth beneath is quaking.

Call forth Solomon's seal,
Cleanse my feet!
Hot coals lie beneath each prancing step.
Bring me the wormwood
So I can see clearly again,
Your casketed face, unknown being.

Oh, you dare to sing this morning song.
You dare to diminish anguish,
Disturbing purple ponds that seize earthbound oxygen
And make me breathless to face the day.
Again I ask,
Little bird, why are you singing?

BONNIE MCCALL

My Head Is on Your Shoulder Now

The evening comes earlier
Now that the Autumnal Equinox has passed.
The triumphant sun
Journeys its daily course
Across melted cerulean heavens
And anchors its hold on a distant skyline,
Like a sailor coming home forever.

In quietude now, birds vanish perches.
The minds of men stop their endless inundation of words,
Wrapping newsfeeds up in their living rooms
While I drift outside in the crisp harvest air,
Hoping for a high priestess to appear.
Perhaps she will wave a wand of wondrous power,
Sweeping me away to your land,
Your resting place,
Your final shore.

There is a heavy weight I feel, left center.
It keeps rhythmic tides flowing
Through the thoroughfares of my soul.
Though heavy, it insists on beating.
Breathing in the smell of leaves burning,
I am reminded of past November days.
Time collapses into previous decades,
Like an old-fashioned reel of film laid out for inspection,
Your life story.

I peer down at it and want to be shrunken small,
Into just one frame standing beside you.

You will carry me home now
With my head upon your shoulder.

I Am the Sound

The low pitch of your voice,
Is a melancholy sound,
Like falling leaves from the tree,
When the wind is not blowing
And an unseen weight is on your back.

Too many days of inside weather,
While outside you carried a smile.
Too many walks on a tightrope
Between buildings that do not bend.

Too many times softly spoken
For ears that refuse to be open.
Too many goodbyes forgotten
The day that your face disappeared.

Too many new things to remember.
Too little help came your way.
It's just understood that you will function
When nothing comes back as okay.

Today you are me and I am you.
I understand the sadness in your voice.
And love the sound of leaves falling down,
Without worry.
It is alright with me
If you silently cry one more time.
I am the sound of falling tears.

BONNIE MCCALL

December Chill

December chill sinks deep into my soul.
I am free
And blown easily by the wind,
Like the snow,
Drifting,
Deeply yearning to pile layer on layer,
So that I am unseen and no longer vulnerable,
Wrapping myself with yesterday's weather.

Falling facedown with frozen emotion,
There are no snow angels here.
Just fallen crystals of time,
Slowing me.

I am blinded by the fact that in a few days,
The beauty of this landscape will be dirty slush
Inside my soul,
Vulnerable to the deception of warmth.

Snow

Hopelessness enveloped me, then the snow came.
White crystalline flakes
Fall from the woven fabric matrix above.
Mathematically, each small, soft flake is created
Individually and beautifully, constructed by unseen gentle power,
Quietly, without human intervention.

Falling to dry earth, tumbling downward,
Piling,
Blanketing the ground with clean, cool freshness.
Empty tree limbs are dressed in lace,
Delighted to bring beauty to the frozen landscape.

Beneath the snow,
Earth warms, crystals melt,
Water quenches a thirsty terrain,
Life-giving spirits baptize the dry brown soil.

My inner child flies to the sea of white,
Lies down in its glory, wanting only to create upon this landscape
An imprint
Washed in snow-white elegance,
As if an angel, transported by sheer joy,
Ascended to the matriculated sky,
Searching for love.
She is so thirsty to fly freely from this worldly terrain.

Snow
Melts me into you,
So far above.

BONNIE MCCALL

Pine Tree

Tall, tortuous trunk,
Old, looming pine,
Watching and waiting over the empty skeleton
Of the uninhabited house next door.

I see you daily and wonder why you continue to guard
That obvious, lonely existence.
No known energy flows in or out,
Webs and curtains still the windows.
Even the neighborhood rabbits
Seem to avoid the overgrown bushes.

I see your faithfulness, though.
You lean in toward its roof and frame,
Like an angelic being,
Guiding, protecting,
Spreading green wings to shelter
And throw as many finger branches as possible for shade
From elements.

You must remember the previous inhabitants.
Are you still looking, waiting for them to come home?
Do you remember the energy of past years?
Was there light and frolic inside, a gaiety that lingered?
Or was there a darkness that brooded and pushed everyone away?

Are you sighing in the wind?
Do those green branches display your empathy?
Are the ones filled with faded, parched needles
Carrying on the business of living for the good of nature,
Balancing out the death
Of a home gone silent?

Another Spring

Light, upon broken, muddied earth,
Opens the day earlier now,
Notifying all that time is calling
To a higher, more urgent place.
"Please start now," she beckons,
While the earth is awakening
And needy seeds must be planted.

Chirping birds call out.
I have not heard them burst open the morning
For many months.
Music of life, the promised land is called to newness,
A new flower must bloom.
A new soul must emerge.

A quick memory floods my mind.
The silent past,
Falling skies, frozen thoughts, shadows that linger then disappear
Into the moon, all alone in the sky.
But they say winter is now gone,
And the wind that blew so hard on your back has retreated.

Sky, shrouded in soft gray fabric
Swirls above,
Opening methodically, minute by minute.
Temperature warming,
Only a whisper of breeze remains to kiss my cheek.

I am feeling the loss of you
As the air silences.

Forgiveness is now the fertilizer that causes the broken seed to sprout.
Love is now the catalyst to make me face the spring that calls me.
One more time, I am emptiness in the growing green of spring.

BONNIE MCCALL

No Fear

Gray slate hovers over me
Like an umbrella, a protective shield,
My warrior shield.
Thick gilded metal reflecting, deflecting
This sphere of earthly concerns.
I am a treasure chest, my crest a seal of beauty, safety, eternal bliss!
I have faced death, and it does not exist.

So powerful is the zephyr that I ride upon
That I can traverse the gap between here and now.
I am a goddess of light.
I aspire to freedom from the terror pricking at my children.
Omnipotence guides all creatures of the morning
To gather around me.
We safely play sweet songs.

Chanting with my myriads of fairies,
You heard my echoing call.
You came to me, and we danced on death together!
My armor is unnecessary now.
Together, powerful like a supernova,
We rest.

The grass is soft with dew.
We rest in the sweetness of safety,
Having known each other for eons.
An eternity of secrets are shared,
As the softness of our hands mold together.
Your eyes are blue-green as Giverny, glistening and pure.

I am a water lily, floating on time.
I no longer fear death.

There Is a Place

There is a place,
Soft and misty,
Quiet,
Blissful,
Radiant.
It is a garden lush with orchids of infinite depth.
Sadness, a free expression,
Leads to comfort
Where the warm blanket of the universe
Engulfs all who seek refuge and shelter.

We are like butterflies that flutter
In and out,
Flirting with humanity,
Weaving a pattern with two wings,
Ever-engaging, ever-changing,
The dynamic force of energy unceasing!
Duality was our learning place,
And oneness is our lesson.

No more tremulous doubt.
No more to figure out.
No more letting go.
It is our DNA.
It is already known.

We already knew each other.
We fluttered here, all glorious,
With wings spread wide
And hope as high as mountains.

Our love engulfs the breeze that caresses and soothes.
We already knew that we could conquer this dance with eternity,
So take my hand as we ascend to the place called home.

Swirling Sea

Swirling sea,
Wash over me.
Wondrous waves, blue and gray,
Clear silk enhances vision,
Melting my soul with endless serenity.
So small am I among these droplets,
So huge the body of knowledge.

I am afloat,
Like a piece of driftwood,
That even in its search has beauty.
Even with the imperfection of the unfinished, splintered surface
With gaps and holes,
Aimless and impulsive,
I know that I am drifting toward you.

We echoed each other with silence.
Hours of knowing without words,
Painfully, the reckoning came.
I knew you were lost and hurting.
My spirit sent a song to you.
When you've got hardship, I've got hardship, too.

The ocean swept over you
Abandoning this ship with the knowledge
That rocking the boat sometimes saves us.
I drift toward the endless comforting stars,
Their light calling names every minute,
So bright and loud that I forget my post on this driftwood
And float quietly, finally,
Above the unanchored ocean, waves flopping and jostling around,
Above the clamor of others who are searching,
Above earthly intentions.

You send clouds to embrace me,
And I am finally home.

BONNIE MCCALL

The Game

The August breeze came down the street,
Dressed in a shocking coolness
That made the people
Who walked quietly to their cars early in the day shiver.

It is the date, exactly one year ago
That you blew away to another place without me.
It was the day that summer released its hot, humid air,
Transitioning to an early autumn,
Hot and cold belying one another.

Autumn was my favorite season,
Memories of visiting you on college campus,
Students with books abreast,
Woolen hats dancing on heads of flattened, static hair.
The smoky smell of fresh burnt leaves,
And crisp caramel apples fill the air.

I know I asked you your favorite season,
But I don't remember what you said.
How could I not know nor recall that simple fact,
Yet know some of your deepest secrets?

Our friendship did not depend on weathered seasons,
Yet it turned upon the weathered seasons of our souls,
Entangled with similar sufferings,
Laughing and crying together about the nonsense
Experienced in this game of life.

It's my move next and the chessboard feels empty.
The Queen is protected, but now you are gone.

Your number is still on my phone,
And the 10th day of August feels chilly to me.
My fingers blue from lack of circulation,

A coolness that intensifies my need to hear your voice.

The silence of this day roars through my mind like a lion.
If I talk about you, the tears still flow
As if it were yesterday that we cried together,
When I knew and you knew that we would say goodbye,
A game unfinished.
I could not be there.
Well, the other players blocked my move.

Did you know how much I wanted to see you again?
You won the game.

BONNIE MCCALL

Goodbye

While the wind blows slowly over my unpolished face,
Tossing my hair in a current of unstyled sadness,
The sun sets softly on my slanted shoulders,
No longer sending shimmering, youthful rays,
Just quiet silhouettes of days ending,
Suspending time.

I return briefly to the mental image:
A green park, a bench that is swallowed up, gone now.
You sat with me, hovering concernedly,
Serving me with counsel
For things not understood inside my soul.

I have returned to that image of you
Over and over this year.
The words that you said never registered with me.
The only sound that I heard was
You sitting with the silence of me.

Every day since you left
A memory, a thought,
A leaf blows past, a butterfly,
Sachets upon the breeze.
And you appear,
Sitting in the car beside me or on a wooden, iron-framed bench.
The whisper of your voice echoes in tranquility.
And I wait,
Knowing that we will talk again.
No rocking of the boat, just keeping the peace,
Like childhood days gone by.

So forgive me if I set a date within my
Eternal Akashic record
To meet with you
Quietly on a bench
With the wind blowing gently on our tattered souls,
As I honor our journey
And never say goodbye.

Finding You

I must fly to the stars.
Please meet me there!
To gather fragments of light,
Bring them back in a woven basket
Made of silken threads and platinum filaments,
Filaments so thin and shiny, woven throughout
So that my basket is strong and invincible.

I will zoom to the outermost realms of the galaxy,
Light and carefree,
Visiting places that men could not comprehend, known only to me,
So my fragmented heart,
Broken, fragile, but free,
Could find its lighted pathway back home to me.

I will gather each fragment,
And as I do,
The light that it builds
Will spill over to you.
The darkness around me means nothing.
I am light as a feather,
And with gratitude say, "The dark night is over."

Acknowledgments

Penning poetry from the heart is a collaborative journey. I am deeply grateful to those who supported and inspired me along the way.

Thank you to Jennifer Bright, who became an invaluable source of encouragement after entering my life. Noelle, my talented artist, assisted me every step of the way in bringing this chapbook to life. To my husband, David, who continued to support my endeavors despite poetry not being his cup of tea—I am forever thankful.

My appreciation also extends to Pamela, who found melody in my words, and Melissa, who supported me even when my verses were not easily understood. And to Katja, my youngest daughter, your love for poetry's spirit and the life that breathes within every being is a continuous inspiration.

A special acknowledgment to my late brother, who opened my spirit to the power of words. His memory fuels my passion for providing solace and hope through my poetry.

About the Artist

Noëlle McCall graduated with a BFA in visual arts and art history from SUNY Potsdam. She lives in a small town in Pennsylvania with her partner and a lovably anxious dog named Samwise. When she is not driving to a Stars on Ice show or a concert by The Mountain Goats, you can find her writing and drawing.

About the Author

Born in the rolling hills of western Pennsylvania, Bonnie McCall has always been a survivor, drawing strength from the world around her. Throughout her life, she's experienced the power and beauty of words as they flowed through her mind in poetic clusters. Often, she didn't pause to transcribe them, trusting that these words originated from a sacred source.

Balancing her passion for language with her commitment to helping others, Bonnie dedicated much of her life to working as a nurse—bringing healing and hope to those in need. When her brother passed away, she turned to writing as a means of healing her own heart. Through these heartfelt poems, she hopes to provide comfort and peace to those who are also navigating life's difficult moments.